Overcoming
FEAR

30-DAY DEVOTIONAL

THANK YOU!

We'd like to thank all of the Proverbs 31 Ministries authors who contributed to our 30-Day Devotional: Overcoming Fear. Our goal was to meet women where they're at in life, and we know fear is an important topic for everyone.

Thank you to all who made this project possible. Your words are making a difference around the world!

The Proverbs 31 Ministries Team

TABLE OF CONTENTS

Have I not commanded you?
Be strong and courageous.
Do not be afraid;
do not be discouraged,
for the Lord your
God will be with you
wherever you go.

JOSHUA 1:9

Dear friend,

We all face "what ifs," both big and small: *What if my marriage falls apart? What if people reject me? What if I fail? What if my child gets sick?*

It seems there's so much to be afraid of in life. And sadly, fear can hold many of us back from loving others fully, from pursuing our dreams, and from living out God's calling on our lives. Yet God's plan for us is to live with His peace and confidence. But how do we find that?

At Proverbs 31 Ministries, we understand, and we're learning with you. So that's why we put together the *30-Day Devotional Overcoming Fear*. Read each day's devotion and then use the "Reflect and Respond" sections at the end of each devotion to hide God's Word in your heart, and to thank God for who He is and for what He's doing in your life.

Finally, thank you for purchasing this journal. Your support helps our ministry to continue offering free resources like our *Encouragement for Today* devotions, Online Bible Studies, and the First 5 app to women all around the world.

Sweet blessings,

The Proverbs 31 Ministries Team

Day 1: When God Hurts Your Feelings • LYSA TERKEURST

"I know what it is to be in need, and I know what it is to have plenty. I have learned the secret of being content in any and every situation, whether well fed or hungry, whether living in plenty or in want. I can do everything through him who gives me strength." (Philippians 4:12-13 NIV)

Has God ever hurt your feelings? I'll be honest, sometimes I'll read those verses from Philippians listed above and think to myself, "This is a tough pill to swallow."

Content in any and every situation?

Really?

A few years ago my daughter was a state champion gymnast. To see her do gymnastics was like looking at God smile. She was beautiful, graceful, and captivating to watch.

Then one night while practicing for one of the largest tournaments she'd ever competed in, she fell. It was a move she'd done hundreds of times with the greatest of ease. But this time something went terribly wrong and that one mistake ended her gymnastic dreams.

We spent a year going from doctor to doctor only to be told she'd never be able to support the weight of her body on her injured shoulder again.

I'll be honest, this was a tough pill to swallow. Watching a 14-year-old girl wrestle with the fact that her dreams were stripped from her doesn't exactly lend itself to feelings of contentment.

Now, I know in the grand scheme of life, people face much worse situations. But in her world, this was huge.

It was so tempting to want to wallow in the "why" questions and tell God He'd hurt our feelings.

Why did this happen?

Why didn't You stop this God?

Why weren't my prayers answered?

Have you ever been there? Have you ever had a big situation in your life where you just couldn't process why God would allow this to happen? Or maybe even a small annoyance like losing your keys or having a flat tire on a morning you really needed to be somewhere.

It's so tempting to wallow in the why whispers. He may ask us to talk less and listen more so we can be more intentional with our prayers.

Maybe God wants to interrupt your prayers, too. He doesn't want you to stop praying, but instead be faithful to press pause and start praising.

Dear Lord, help me examine each situation I am currently praying about, so I can praise You for what You are already doing. In Jesus' name, amen.

Asking why is perfectly normal. Asking why isn't unspiritual. However, if asking this question pushes us farther from God rather than drawing us closer to Him, it is the wrong question.

If asking the why question doesn't offer hope, what will?

The what question.

In other words: "Now that this is my reality, what am I supposed to do with it?"

Philippians 4:8, "Finally brothers, whatever is true, whatever is noble, whatever is right, whatever is pure, whatever is lovely, whatever is admirable—if anything is excellent or praiseworthy—think about such things" (NIV).

I like to call this verse "directions on where to park my mind."

And that's exactly what Ashley has had to do with her dashed gymnastics dreams. Instead of wallowing in why did this happen, I've had to help her say:

This is my reality, now what am I going to do with it?

What can I learn from this?

What part of this is for my protection?

What other opportunities could God be providing?

What maturity could God be building into me?

Switching from the why to the what questions paves the road to parking our minds in a much better place.

Is it always easy? Nope.

But is it a way to find a perspective beyond situations where we feel God has allowed something in our lives we don't understand and we absolutely don't like? Yes. I pray this helps you today.

Dear Lord, I want to process everything I face in life through the filter of Your love. I know You love me. But sometimes it's just hard to understand the circumstances that come my way. I find myself consumed with trying to figure things out rather than looking for Your perspective and trusting You. Thank You for this new way to look at things. In Jesus' name, amen.

REFLECT AND RESPOND:

Am I afraid to have honest conversations with God about how I really feel about some of my circumstances?

....

....

How might it be helpful to really talk to God about things that hurt me?

....

....

Why is it helpful to ask what now, instead of wallowing in the why questions?

....

....

Day 2: Jesus in the Fog • TRACIE MILES

"Give all your worries and cares to God, for he cares about you." (1 Peter 5:7 NLT)

- -

I was full of emotions as my husband and I drove to pick up my dad for surgery. A knot formed in the pit of my stomach. I was worried about the extensive surgery that he would face later that morning. I was anxious, knowing that the possibility existed to receive very bad news from the surgeon. I was fretting over various circumstances, and as I prayed for God to intervene, I began to feel hot tears stinging my eyes.

But then, through those tears, I saw something in the fog.

Due to the dense, heavy fog, my husband was driving slowly when I noticed the figure in the distance, walking straight towards us. I thought it was odd for anyone to be walking outside on such a cool and foggy morning, but as we got closer my eyes widened and my heart began to pound.

This figure began to resemble a silhouette of someone I recognized—someone who should not be standing in the middle of the road on a misty, foggy morning. As we approached this person in front of my dad's house, I noticed that he had on baggy tan pants, a soft white shirt, and was wearing no shoes. He appeared to be in his mid-thirties with brown wavy hair and a full, neatly kept beard. He looked peaceful and kind.

He looked exactly like Jesus.

My heart skipped a beat. My thoughts were racing. My intellectual mind knew that Jesus would not be standing in the middle of a road on a foggy day in a small beach town in North Carolina, but my heart told me that He was there. I could not take my eyes off of this person as chill bumps flushed my body from head to toe. As we drove slowly past him, this man in the fog made direct eye contact with me and a sweet, gentle smile washed over his face.

For those brief moments it felt as if I was looking into the eyes of Jesus, and a feeling of peace flooded through me. It was as if His holy peace penetrated my heart and assured me that, regardless of the outcome, everything would be okay. Throughout that day at the hospital I could not get the man in the fog out of my head, and I truly felt as if I had experienced a Jesus encounter.

Now I am not saying that I actually saw Jesus, of course, but I do believe that He divinely designed that meeting in the road, and that He used a sign that I would recognize as Him to saturate my heart with the reminder that He really does walk among us. God knew I needed to know that He saw my daddy, understood my fears, and cared. He also knew I really needed to see Him that day.

Throughout life, we are all faced with fears of the unknown and personal problems that seem hopeless or scary, and it is so easy to get caught up in our emotions, forgetting to look for God. In some situations we may even find ourselves wondering if God is really aware of our problems and doubt if He really cares, but 1 Peter 5:7 is a sweet reminder that He is aware, He does care, and He is with us.

Life can make us feel like we are in a fog—a fog so dense and heavy that it seems nearly impossible to feel or see God at all. But even if we can't see Him, He has promised to be with us if we surrender our hearts and sincerely seek out His face. Then as we walk with Him and sincerely believe He is walking with us, we enter into a place to receive His provisions, His blessings, His comfort, and His peace.

When we prepare our hearts to experience Him, He will prepare our eyes to see Him.

Dear Lord, I seek Your face with my whole heart. Help me to see You in a special way. In Jesus' name, amen.

- -

REFLECT AND RESPOND:

Have I had a hard time seeing God in the midst of my life lately?

....

....

....

....

....

....

Are emotions and doubts clouding my vision?

....

....

....

....

....

....

Do I fully trust God to work in my situations?

....

....

....

Day 3: *When Fear Paralyzes Your Faith* • RENEE SWOPE

"'Do not fear, for I have redeemed you; I have summoned you by name; you are mine. When you pass through the waters, I will be with you; and when you pass through the rivers, they will not sweep over you. When you walk through the fire, you will not be burned; the flames will not set you ablaze.'" (Isaiah 43:1b-2 NIV)

I crawled into bed and slipped under a blanket of fear. My husband was out of town for work, and I was afraid to go to sleep. Fear had become a constant companion during his nights away. I knew I needed to trust God, but I didn't.

Instead, I went through the motions of what good Christians do: I prayed, read Scripture and taped Bible verses on sticky notes to my lamp and bedside table. But then I also put a phone under my pillow and a neighborhood directory beside my bed.

The next night, I took it a step further by putting toys on the stairs—to trip possible burglars. I brought my children into my room to sleep there as well, and moved the dresser in front of our bedroom door.

Although I thought I was controlling my circumstances, fear had taken control of me. Frustrated that I still couldn't sleep, I opened the Bible and read a familiar passage, found in today's key verse:

"'Do not fear, for I have redeemed you; I have summoned you by name; you are mine. When you pass through the waters, I will be with you; and when you pass through the rivers, they will not sweep over you. When you walk through the fire, you will not be burned; the flames will not set you ablaze'" (Isaiah 43:1b-2).

As I read each word slowly, God showed me something I'd never seen: My fears were like flames and my efforts to protect myself were like gasoline. Every attempt to ease my fears was like dousing fuel on the fire, and now it was consuming me.

Gently, the Holy Spirit reminded me that God had not given me a spirit of fear but a spirit "of power and of love and of a sound mind" (2 Timothy 1:7b, NKJV).

Suddenly I knew the only way to overcome my fear and walk in faith was to walk through what I feared the most. I had to put away the props in which I'd placed my faith and go to bed trusting God, realizing that even if my fears came true, He would be with me.

I crawled out of bed and put everything away. The dresser went back in place. My kids went back to their rooms and I went to sleep without my phone under my pillow. And that night, I slept better than I had in weeks.

Fear loses its power when we actively trust God more than what we fear.

Let's ask God to show us what we are afraid of. What is paralyzing our faith and keeping us from living confidently in His peace and freedom? And then let's give God a chance to come through for us as we courageously walk through our fears, holding God's hand and trusting His heart to lead, protect and preserve us each step of the way.

Dear God, help me walk through my fears by facing them instead of being paralyzed by them. I want to take Your hand and trust Your heart with all that is within me. Give me courage today to take the first step. In Jesus' name, amen.

REFLECT AND RESPOND:

What fears paralyze your faith or hinder your everyday life?

....

....

....

....

....

....

Ask God to show you one step to take today to walk through a fear that keeps you from trusting Him completely.

Day 4: Choose Where You Will Stand • TRACIE MILES

"Be on your guard; stand firm in the faith; be men of courage; be strong." (1 Corinthians 16:13 NIV)

Several years ago, I began playing tennis and became a member of a competitive team. Each week the team attends a practice clinic with our tennis professional to learn new techniques and strategies. He is always full of great tips and advice to help us improve our game, but one particular week he said something that really stuck in my mind.

He discussed the importance of court position—where we stand on the court could determine whether or not we keep the ball in play and if we win the point. Then he said that although we could not control what was going on in the court, we could always control where we stand.

I thought about how that statement is applicable not only to tennis, but to life. You see, even though we can't control what happens in the world, we can always control where we stand on issues of righteousness and integrity. Where we choose to stand will be evidence of the role that we are allowing God to play in our lives.

For example, we have no power over the sex, drugs, language, and violence on TV, but we can choose whether we watch it or not. We have no power over the content of the movies coming out in the theaters, or how lenient the ratings are, but we can choose what we allow ourselves or our children to see. We can stand for purity.

We have no power to control the beliefs and actions of other people. We cannot control the downfall of morals in our society. We cannot control the decisions that Congress makes, which new laws are put into place, escalating gas prices, politics in the workplace, questionable practices in corporations, liberal tolerance, foreign affairs, war, or the state of the economy.

In fact, sometimes it may seem that we have no control over certain situations in our own lives, much less the things happening in the world. But there is good news—we always have the choice to choose where we will stand in the game of life.

Proverbs 20:5 says, "Knowing what is right is like deep water in the heart; a wise person draws from the well within" (MSG). That is really where court position begins—in the heart. If our faith is strong and grounded we'll be able to pull from that wisdom when faced with opportunities to choose where to stand, knowing that the power of God within us will empower us to make good decisions.

Our only hope in fighting this battle of good versus evil—in our hearts and in this broken world— is to be prepared to stand tall and firm for Christ, despite what the opposition may bring.

You know, life is a lot like a tennis court. We each have our side. We try to stay on the right side, but sometimes the balls that get thrown at us pull us in the wrong direction. Other times they are difficult to defend, cause us to stumble, or throw us off track. But if we choose the right court position to begin with, that is to stay on God's side and choose Him as our partner, we are much more likely to exercise the power we have within us. Drawing deep from the well of God's wisdom in our hearts, we can do the right thing.

There are times when standing up for our faith may cause us to lose the popularity contest, but it will allow others to see God in us. And, there may even be times when our court position speaks louder than words ever could.

Where will you stand today?

Dear Lord, help me have the strength and faith to stand up for what is right when I am faced with opposition, and not be swayed by the pressures in a fallen world. Help me live a life that glorifies You, instead of just taking the easy road and going along with the crowd. In Jesus' name, amen.

REFLECT AND RESPOND:

What opportunities have you recently had to stand up for truth? How did you do?

....

....

....

....

....

....

If you were faced with opposition to God's truth in some way today, would you be prepared to stand up for Him?

....

....

....

....

....

....

....

Day 5: Will You Give Me Your Son? • GLYNNIS WHITWER

"And she made a vow, saying 'LORD Almighty, if you will only look on your servant's misery and remember me, and not forget your servant but give her a son, then I will give him to the LORD for all the days of his life, and no razor will ever be used on his head.'" (1 Samuel 1:11 NIV)

As my arms wrapped tighter around my son, I squeezed my eyes hoping the hot tears would stop. Forcing a smile I knew he'd want to see, I released him and stepped back on the airport sidewalk.

Despite my efforts, tears dripped down my cheeks. I grinned and shrugged, unable to speak. Thankfully my son's gentle teasing helped get past the awkwardness of the goodbye. With a final hug, my 19-year-old left for a mission trip to China.

Having children willing to serve God was my heart's desire before they were born. It was what I've prayed for since they were small. And it is what I have worked toward for years. I just didn't know it was going to stretch my faith so much.

You see, long ago my husband and I dedicated our children to the Lord, and we raised them to serve God. I was thrilled at my son's decision to go on a mission trip, but the reality of releasing him to God's calling felt like a piece of my heart was being torn away.

It was so much easier to dedicate my children to God during the three years my husband and I struggled with infertility. Each time I read the story of Hannah and her struggle with infertility in 1 Samuel 2, my heart leapt in hope. Just as she pledged her child to the Lord if He would only give her one, I was willing to do the same.

It was also easier to dedicate my children to God once we finally had them, while they were wrapped safely in my arms.

But standing at the airport, there was a fragile part of me that wanted to take back that offer. Fears rose up. My son is so adventurous, what if something happened? What if I never saw him again?

I tried to put the fears aside, but hours after our final goodbye, I still had a crumpled tissue in my hand. It was then I heard God speak to my heart. It was unmistakably Him—I'd never ask myself this question: "Will you give Me your son?"

By that time my son was on a plane, so the question seemed pointless. But what I wanted to say was this: "Well, now that You've asked—the answer is no, I've changed my mind about all that dedication stuff I said years ago."

In the weeks since that day, I've often wondered why God would ask that question since He didn't really need my permission. I've come to believe it's because He knows the influence a mother has on her children, even when they're grown. With words spoken or withheld, tone of voice, and emotional and financial support (or lack thereof), a mother can influence her children's obedience to God's call at every age.

And in my case, God knows my fears have affected my children. Ten years earlier when my oldest son wanted to go on an international mission trip, my fears stopped him. At that time, I thought he was too young and the destination too far. Without my active support, his plans fizzled.

Over the years, God has helped me overcome that fear time and time again, and eventually that same son went on other mission trips. Every time I've released my tight grip on my children to obey God, my faith has grown. Apparently my faith needed to grow again, hence God's heart check that day: "Will you give Me your son?"

Gripping my soggy tissue, I whispered a shaky "Yes." Hoping it was good enough, but sensing it wasn't, I answered again, this time with confidence: "Yes! You can have my son!"

Immediately peace started to grow in my heart as I turned my eyes from my own situation to His plan for my son. Peace and joy continued to grow stronger each day.

Sometimes I wish I were one of those mothers who never deals with fear. They seem so confident and faith-filled. But I've learned when I give God my weaknesses, His power is displayed and His kingdom is advanced. So in spite of a bit of trembling, and a few tears, I'm going to say yes each time God asks if He can have one of my children.

Heavenly Father, thank You for loving me in spite of my weakness. I want to trust You more and confess the times fear has held me back. Help me to be honest with You and receive Your strength. In Jesus' name, amen.

REFLECT AND RESPOND:

Fear has the power to stop us from obeying God's calling for ourselves and in how we support others in their calling. How has fear affected your obedience?

....

....

....

....

....

....

....

....

....

Day 6: Where Can I Find JOY? • WENDY BLIGHT

"Dear brothers and sisters, when troubles come your way, consider it an opportunity for great joy." (James 1:2 NLT)

My daughter's journey with scoliosis was a heartbreaking time for me as a mother. There were days I couldn't see past Lauren's extreme physical pain and my wandering heart questioned, why hasn't God healed her yet?

Through those years, I struggled. I felt empty—void of hope, void of joy. I knew what God's Word said about joy: "Dear brothers and sisters, when troubles come your way, consider it an opportunity for great joy" (James 1:2 NLT). But in the midst of Lauren's circumstances, her broken heart and wounded body, it was hard to follow that command.

How could I obey this scripture and find joy when someone I loved was in such pain? God graciously answered the cry of my heart by revealing to me these three words: Jesus Only You. I noticed the first letter of each of those words spelled joy. And it clicked with me. Jesus is our joy!

When God says in James 1:2 to consider trials as opportunities for joy, He's not talking about the joy found in earthly things. Circumstances turning out how we desire, possessions and positions, and even good health only offer happiness. They are temporary. What God longs for us to have is deep, lasting joy found in Jesus.

The King James Version says we are to "count it all joy" when we walk through trials. This word "count" means "evaluate."

When trials come, we must evaluate them in light of God's truths and promises. It's not the trial itself we consider a joy. Rather, it's the results that will come from the trial that we consider pure joy.

This involves trusting that God is actively working for our good even in the midst of painful circumstances. And as we trust Him, we will find an inner gladness rooted not in our circumstances, but in the reality of the living God who transcends our circumstances.

After years of praying, asking God to heal my daughter, He did. It still hurts to remember the excruciating pain Lauren suffered. But God was and is faithful. God didn't heal my girl in the miraculous way I was expecting. Instead, she endured a seven-hour surgery to place two rods in her spine. She missed nearly six weeks of school and labored through months of relearning how to sit and walk and move. She had to quit competitive cheerleading. But in and through that time, God did a new thing.

Looking back, I can see how He held us up, deepened Lauren's faith, and drew our family closer to each other. In real and personal ways, God showed us His tender, loving care. And He taught me the meaning of true joy.

Jesus alone is the source of our joy.

When discouragement comes and you feel you cannot take one more step, remember these three words, Jesus Only You!

Jesus came so that I—so that you—can experience His joy fully and completely in us through any and all circumstances.

Heavenly Father, thank You for Jesus. Thank You for the joy that is ours in Him. Every time our thoughts turn to our hurt, cause our pain to bring us back to joy—Jesus Only You. In Jesus' name, amen.

REFLECT AND RESPOND:

What does it mean to be filled with the joy of the Lord?

....

....

....

....

....

....

What keeps you from receiving the fullness of His joy? Memorize and personalize James 1:2 so that you can recall it the next time you walk through a difficult trial and feel the absence of joy.

....

....

....

....

....

....

Day 7: Pause and Breathe • TRACIE MILES

"So we will not fear when earthquakes come and the mountains crumble into the sea." (Psalm 46:2 NLT)

Recently as I was waiting to board a plane, I felt a little twinge of anxiety.

I looked tentatively at the other passengers at the gate, wondering if any posed a threat. I found myself reading their faces, looking at their carry-on bags and speculating if anything dangerous might have slipped through.

You see, the horrific events of previous months were heavy on my heart. As the news broadcasts so many calamities, innocent lives lost and people injured, it's easy to harbor fear and wonder: What's happening to our world? Why are people so evil? Can we ever feel safe?

In that airport terminal, my mind was on the verge of drifting to a thousand what-ifs and whys when I remembered God's promise in Psalm 46. As I allowed His truth to sink in, I paused to take comfort in the fact that there was no need to fear, because no matter what, God is with us.

Verses 1-3 assure us that "God is our refuge and strength, always ready to help in times of trouble. So we will not fear when earthquakes come and the mountains crumble into the sea. Let the oceans roar and foam. Let the mountains tremble as the waters surge!" Interlude

God is our Protector. He is where we find strength to get through tough times when we are afraid. When the earth crumbles, floods abound, avalanches roar, tornados threaten—He is our refuge.

Yet, sometimes in the face of tragedy and heartache, we question God, doubting His promise of protection. Although God does have the authority and ability to protect us from every trouble, sometimes He uses the trials we go through to teach us, purify us and draw us closer to Him. Although at times it may seem that God has not protected us in the way we need or desire, we can rest in knowing that He is protecting us in the way He knows is best for us to learn to fully depend on Him.

Psalm 46:4-7 says, "A river brings joy to the city of our God, the sacred home of the Most High. God dwells in that city; it cannot be destroyed. From the very break of day, God will protect it. The nations are in chaos, and their kingdoms crumble! God's voice thunders, and the earth melts! The Lord of Heaven's Armies is here among us; the God of Israel is our fortress." Interlude

While I love the ocean, I don't long to dig my toes in the shorelines when there's a storm. But I wouldn't mind sitting on the banks of a peaceful river, even during a rainstorm. Just like the calm, flowing waters of a river, God weaves His peace and provision throughout our lives even in chaos.

Psalm 46:8-11 says, "Come, see the glorious works of the LORD: See how he brings destruction upon the world. He causes wars to end throughout the earth. He breaks the bow and snaps the spear; he burns the shields with fire. Be still, and know that I am God! I will be honored by every nation. I will be honored throughout the world. The Lord of Heaven's Armies is here among us; the God of Israel is our fortress." Interlude

Although the world is in disarray, God is still God. He is still on the throne. Still mighty. Still faithful. Still sovereign.

In all three sections in this passage, each one ends with the word Interlude. The definition of interlude is to pause, break, breathing space, or rest.

When we pause to focus on the truth that God is God, we find rest.

If fear has been creeping into your heart lately, pause and remember that God is your protector; His presence is with you, and He is in the highest position of authority over this broken world. Ask Him to settle the anxiousness in your heart. Then, just breathe.

Dear Lord, thank You for being a safe place to flee, for always providing peace in the face of anxieties. Fill us with joy. In Jesus' name, amen.

REFLECT AND RESPOND:

Consider what fears, whether valid or imagined, have been burdening your heart lately. Search God's Word for a verse that specifically addresses that fear(s).

....

....

....

....

....

....

....

....

....

....

....

Day 8: Undignified Worship • GLYNNIS WHITWER

"...It was before the LORD who chose me rather than your father or anyone from his house when he appointed me ruler over the LORD's people Israel—I will celebrate before the LORD. I will become even more undignified than this..." (2 Samuel 6:21-22a NIV)

I grew up in a traditional church, singing traditional hymns. Being a Christian was very matter-of-fact for me. I was a Christian in the same way I would have told you I was a student.

Nothing much changed in our little church. Every Sunday, faithful men and woman of God taught Sunday school, served on committees and made lemonade, coffee, and cookies for after-church fellowship. It was a wonderful experience and I grew up loving God's Word, His church, and its people.

When I was a high schooler in the late '70s, I was introduced to Christian "rock and roll." Being in Arizona, we got overflow from the California Jesus movement, and were familiar with many of the bands coming on the scene. I heard songs by Keith Green, Second Chapter of Acts, and Phil Keaggy. These songs depicted a faith in God that was passionate and alive. Something stirred within me as I listened to their music over and over.

I can still vividly picture myself in a sold-out symphony hall before a live concert as one half of the room yelled, "We love Jesus, yes we do. We love Jesus how 'bout you?" I was on the other side, and we answered as loudly as we could, repeating the challenge. Joy and celebration vibrated through the hall as we shouted, jumped up and down, and waved our arms in the air for love of Jesus.

It was completely undignified and I was completely undone—never to be the same. I knew I wanted a faith like that. I wanted to be so excited about Jesus that it overflowed, and I didn't care what my worship of Him looked like.

A few years ago, I read the story of King David dancing before the Lord. Now there was someone who didn't worry what others thought. David had overseen the return of the ark of the Lord to Jerusalem, and as it neared, he couldn't contain his joy. He replaced his kingly attire with a simple outfit and danced with all his might.

His wife, Michal, watched from the window and didn't approve of David's behavior. She was disgusted with him, and told him so. David wasn't fazed, and responded with words that encourage me today, "It was before the LORD who chose me rather than your father or anyone from his house when he appointed me ruler over the LORD's people Israel—I will celebrate before the LORD. I will become even more undignified than this..." (2 Samuel 6:21-22a).

David was so in tune with God's heart that he was unconcerned with the judgmental comments of others. David's only focus was on worshipping his God with sincerity and abandon.

That is my hope and prayer for myself. I want to let go completely of the fear of man, and worship with uncontained joy. When I am older, too old to dance in some people's opinion,

I hope you'll find my gnarled hands raised, my gray head bobbing, and my body swaying in worship. My kids and grandkids might be embarrassed. But, yes, I will be even more undignified than that for my King.

Dear Lord, King David got it right, and I want to as well. You are worthy of all my worship and adoration. Forgive me for letting the opinions of others influence my worship of You. Help me to focus more on Your majesty, and less on myself. In Jesus' name, amen.

REFLECT AND RESPOND:

Read 2 Samuel 6:14-23. Describe the scene in verses 14 and 15. What are some of the ways people are rejoicing and worshipping God?

....

....

....

....

....

How can David's answer to Michal help us overcome the fear of other's opinions?

....

....

....

....

....

Day 9: Secrets of Success Found in Small Places • LYSA TERKEURST

"Then Moses summoned Bezalel and Oholiab and every skilled person to whom the LORD had given ability and who was willing to come and do the work." (Exodus 36:2 NIV)

The International Christian Retail Show is a big book convention where publishers, authors, agents, media, and bookstore owners all gather to talk shop. Books are pitched. Books are sold. Books are talked about a lot!

I went to this conference years ago when I was a wannabe writer with a book proposal and a dream. A few years ago as I signed pre-release copies of my sixteenth book, *Unglued*, two thoughts went through my mind:

First, thank You, Jesus that people actually came to my book signing. Seriously, there's nothing quite like standing there with a big stack of free promotion books, a permanent marker, and not a soul interested.

So when people actually came, I just wanted to hug every single one of them. Seriously. And if I had lots of money I would've bought them all a steak dinner. I'm not kidding.

The second thought was to look for those desperate for encouragement. Many who came through my book signing line were interested in writing a book. I remember being there. I know what it feels like to walk around with a tote bag full of book proposals and a heart full of nervous hope.

I felt the weight of responsibility to give them the encouragement I so desperately needed when I was in their shoes.

Maybe you are there right now. Maybe you're looking to actively pursue your dreams. Whether it's the hope of being an author or another dream you have bumping around in your heart, here's what I've learned:

Rejection from man doesn't mean rejection from God.

If God has gifted you to write, write! You don't need a book deal to have an impact with your writing. The same is true with other dreams—sing, create, teach, paint, develop—use your gifts right where you are to bless others.

Most overnight success stories are years in the making.

Value the daily discipline of small steps, hard work, honing your craft, and putting in time learning and developing. Take classes. Be mentored. Push through those moments you want to slack off. And do it over and over, year after year.

Be a blessing to others.

Don't keep your work to yourself. Find people who could be blessed with your work. I love to write. But what I love more than writing is seeing my writing help other people. That's where I find the encouragement to push through the hard times.

Expect opposition.

The challenges and disappointments and setbacks are all part of it. And honestly, these hard times serve a great purpose. I've learned much more from my failures in writing than my successes. Use these lessons. Don't waste them by giving up too soon. And remember to glorify Him whether it's a struggle or a success. God uses all things for good.

Look for the small open doors right in front of you.

I always scratch my head when I meet people who tell me they want to write and speak but aren't willing to teach a small Bible study first. If God is calling you to do something, He'll have a door open in front of you. But it might be a small door. Look for the small door and walk through it.

Actually, dance through it with great joy because He will always do great things with people willing to be faithful in the small.

Dear Lord, I praise You for giving me the opportunity to pursue my dreams. I am so humbled that You would call me to serve You. Please help me persevere as I come up against opposition and frustration in the process of saying "yes" to You. In Jesus' name, amen.

REFLECT AND RESPOND:

What goal are you looking to reach?

....

....

....

What small step toward that goal can you take today? Remember, we can't go directly from A-Z. There are many stepping stones along the way.

....

....

....

Surround yourself with a positive support network. Having a strong group of friends/family who will stand with you and be honest with you on your journey is crucial.

....

....

....

Day 10: The Great Wall of Motherhood • KAREN EHMAN

"With your help I can advance against a troop; with my God I can scale a wall." (Psalm 18:29 NIV)

Maybe I could fake being sick.

Or pretend to twist my ankle.

I just have to think of something that will get me out of this! The voice inside my head uttered words of panic.

It was my freshman year of college, and I stood staring at it—a legend on campus. "It" was made of wood and stood tall in the Midwest countryside. They called it simply: "The Wall."

The legend was also a tradition, one that every freshman must take part in: Scale the 10-foot beast, assisted only by the 12-member freshman "core group" led by one upperclassman.

On the backside of the wall was a platform, near the top. Once you were over the wall, you could lower yourself and stand solidly on it. From there, you could reach back over and assist classmates who'd yet to experience the thrill of conquering this wooden monster.

Getting the first person over was the hardest, since no one was on the other side to help to pull them over. Usually the tallest, thinnest and most athletic guy went first. Others hoisted him up on their shoulders, and then he diligently tried to pull himself the rest of the way and topple over to the other side.

Then, one after another, more students lifted, hoisted and pushed until they all made it safely to the other side. I did my part to help others over, but I dreaded my turn. I tried to speak positively to myself: You can do this. Focus. Jump high and grab on tight! But those words of encouragement were drowned out by my thoughts of fear and doubt.

I backed up, took some running steps toward the wall, and then leapt upward with all my might, praying someone's strong arm would catch me.

After a brief moment of panic, I felt the hand of a teammate grab hold of mine and grip tightly. My team then helped me to the top and I gingerly set my feet down on the other side. Sweet relief. We had done it! We had scaled The Wall.

Three years after I was married, I learned I was expecting our first child. I was excited to be carrying a new life. However, I also felt fear as I stared at the massive wall of motherhood I would have to scale—mostly because I thought all the weight was upon my shoulders to be my child's everything.

Caretaker. Provider. Cook. Teacher. Nurse. Social director. Counselor. Coach. And probably something else I hadn't even thought of yet. How in the world was I ever going to be able to do all that?

Thankfully, today's key verse assures us God is near and ready to come to our aid when we are afraid. He can enable us to scale whatever walls of life we face. And now, a quarter-century into my mothering, I see God's hand and help. His hand has been there to guide me as a mom. And

He's sent help in the form of other mothers who've taken my hand and shared both victories and struggles.

I still talk negatively to myself at times, doubting my abilities as a mom and berating myself for the times I blow it. Maybe you do, too. But what if we stopped listening to the voices inside our heads—the ones that fear and fret and worry? What if instead we reached up and out? Up to God who is waiting to tightly grasp our slipping fingers and out to other mothers who have yet to scale the wall?

God is ever faithful. Always nearby. Full of love, compassion and beautiful second chances when we aim high and come up short. God—the perfect parent—will help us parent our children for His glory.

Yes, moms, with God and each other, we can scale the wall of motherhood.

Father, when the voices of fear and doubt threaten to send me into panic, may I hear Your gentle whisper telling me that You are near. Help me reach out to You, and to other moms on this journey, for help in parenting and in life. In Jesus' name, amen.

REFLECT AND RESPOND:

What are your biggest fears as a mom?

....

....

....

....

....

....

How does the imagery of God helping you to scale a wall help you as you face those fears?

....

....

....

....

....

Day 11: I Can't Find the Words • SUZIE ELLER

"Moses was taught all the wisdom of the Egyptians, and he was powerful in both speech and action." (Acts 7:22 NLT)

Have you ever tried to hide from God's call on your life?

Moses did. He fled to the wilderness to get away. The hillside was a comfortable place; one that allowed him to live in obscurity. But God approached Moses as he tended sheep.

When God asked Moses to speak to Pharaoh on His behalf, Moses balked. He felt inadequate. He lifted up his weakness to God and submitted it as an excuse not to do as God asked. "My words get tangled," he said (Exodus 4:10b NLT).

Yet years later in Acts 7:22, we find that Stephen described Moses as powerful in both speech and action.

How could this be? Did he truly struggle with his words, or was it an excuse?

As an Egyptian citizen and adopted member of the royal family, Moses had access to the finest education. As a young man he rose to the rank of prime minister, a task that required him to communicate with others. But Moses is believed to have had a true speech impediment. He struggled to get the words out.

So when God approached Moses to join in an adventure to free His people from slavery, all Moses could think about was his weakness.

When Stephen described Moses, hundreds of years later, he had the advantage of seeing Moses' life span. He had heard of every act of courage and victory. Even in death, the name of Moses was revered among the nation of Israel.

Stephen knew when Moses spoke, though he may have stammered, his words carried weight. The words Moses spoke were described as "life giving" (Acts 7:38 NLT). Moses' words mended arguments, offered justice, negotiated freedom and dispensed wisdom.

Only in hindsight do we see what Moses could not see in the beginning. God wasn't worried about Moses' lack of eloquence, vocabulary or skill, but whether or not Moses trusted God enough to obey.

Where Moses was deficient, God would be sufficient.

Where Moses struggled, God would succeed.

Where Moses was weak, God would be strong.

How many times does God invite us to follow Him into an adventure? Whether it is to be a great mom, or to lead a Bible study, or do anything outside our comfort zone, do we hold up our weaknesses and say, "Sorry, God, I can't," and then point out our weaknesses to Him.

In these instances, "My words get tangled" translates to:

I'm not patient, God, so don't ask me to be a good mom.

I don't like to be in the spotlight, God, so let someone else lead that study.

I'm afraid, God, so don't ask me to [fill in the blank].

When we look past our "tangled words" to His equipping, we find our answer.

What is God asking you to do? Have you been responding with your own version of, "My words get tangled"?

Are you willing to step out in obedience today?

Like Moses, only with hindsight will you one day see how your obedience shaped a child, or a neighbor or a nation.

Or you.

What do you stand to gain as you take the focus off your deficiency to trust in His sufficiency?

Dear Lord, You know my very real weakness. But I am excited to respond to Your voice today. With You all things are possible, so I step out in faith beginning today. In Jesus' name, amen.

- -

REFLECT AND RESPOND:

Abraham was old; Timothy was timid; Jacob was insecure; Peter was impulsive; and Moses had a speech impediment, yet God used each of these people in such a way that their names are etched in history.

Add your name to the list above: I am _____, but with God all things are possible (Mark 10:27).

....

....

....

....

....

....

....

....

....

....

....

Day 12: Planning Funerals That Won't Happen Today • LYSA TERKEURST

"And who of you by being worried can add a single hour to his life?" (Matthew 6:27 NIV)

Years back, my teenage son came to me and asked if he could take his brother and sisters to go get ice cream. How fun! How thoughtful! "Sure," I said. "Let me grab my keys and we'll go." "No, Mom … we sort of want to go just us kids," he quickly replied.

"Oh," and that's about all I could get my mouth to say as my brain started racing and reeling. In my mind's eye pictures started flashing of a terrible accident, a phone call from the police, planning a funeral, and then thinking back to this moment when I could have said no.

And it was that strange sense that everything depended on me and my decisions that made me want to say no. Absolutely not. You will stay home today. You will all stay home forever. I have to keep you safe.

Why do moms do that? Most of us live with this gnawing, aching, terrifying fear that something will happen to one of our children. We carry the pressure that ultimately everything rises and falls on whether or not we can control things. And mentally, too often we plan funerals that won't happen today.

We do it because we know the realities of living in a broken world where car accidents do happen. Tragedy strikes old and young alike. We have no guarantees for tomorrow. And that's really hard on a mama's heart.

I stood at the front window of my house chewing my nails and watching as the entire contents of my mama heart piled into one car.

And I realized I had a choice.

I could run myself ragged creating a false sense of control that can't really protect them. Or, I could ask God to help me make wise decisions and choose to park my mind on the truth.

The truth is: God has assigned each of my kids a certain number of days.

My choices can add to the quality of their life, but not the quantity. They could be at home tucked underneath my wings and if it's their day to go be with Jesus, they will go.

"When I was woven together in the depths of the earth, your eyes saw my unformed body. All the days ordained for me were written in your book before one of them came to be." (Psalm 139:15-16)

Jesus conquered death so we don't have to be afraid of it any longer.

Of course, the death of anyone I love would make me incredibly sad, heartbroken, and dazed with grief. But I don't have to be held captive by the fear of death.

"Since the children have flesh and blood, he [Jesus] too shared in their humanity so that by his death he might destroy him who holds the power of death—that is, the devil—and free those who all their lives were held in slavery by their fear of death." (Hebrews 2:14-15)

Death is only a temporary separation. We will be reunited again.

In 2 Samuel 12, when David's infant child died, he confidently said, "I shall go to him, but he shall not return to me" (v. 23). David knew he would see his child again–not just a faceless soul without an identity, but this child for whom he was longing. He would know him, hold him, kiss him, and the separation death caused would be over.

I certainly don't claim that these truths will help you never ever fear again. But I do hope these truths will settle your heart into a better place.

And the next time my kids go get ice cream together, instead of chewing my nails I'll only pick at them while awaiting their return. See progress? It's good.

Dear Lord, the fear of something happening to one of my children is so raw. And I guess the thing that makes it so hard is I know we live in a broken world and awful things happen to kids. But if I focus on this fear, it will consume me. Instead help me focus on You so I'll only be consumed with Your truth, Your love, Your insights, and Your power. In Jesus' name, amen.

- -

REFLECT AND RESPOND:

The next time you find yourself worrying and getting consumed with fear, see it as a trigger to pray and ask God specifically to use His truth to comfort you.

Think of what commonly triggers your heart to go to those fearful places and pray for Jesus to help you work through these. Ask for Him to show you verses in scripture that will speak truth into your situation.

Day 13: When It All Falls Apart • AMY CARROLL

"It is God who arms me with strength and makes my way perfect." (Psalm 18:32 NIV 1984)

Everything seemed to go wrong at the same time. Instead of having "one of those days," I was having one of those months!

The emotional load in our home increased as my eldest son moved back from college, filling every square inch of our little house with testosterone. My youngest son graduated from high school and then had an accident that would require surgery. My computer crashed, not just once but three times. A spur-of-the-moment trip required hours of unscheduled time. An event I was planning seemed to teeter between success and epic fail. On top of it all, my little dog came down with intestinal issues...I'll spare you the details.

For a time, not one thing in my life seemed to measure up to the picture of perfection in my head. Not my messy home. Not my fearful mothering. Not my unstable professional life. Not my overloaded schedule. Nothing.

I felt weak and overwhelmed. For a woman who loves order, a managed schedule and peace, it's not easy to face times like these. Maybe you've had seasons similar to mine. Perhaps for some of you, it's been even longer—even one of those years—when chaos seems to reign.

As difficult as it is to cope when life gets messy, we can view struggles as a great opportunity to operate in a new way. Rather than focusing on what's wrong and imperfect, we can turn our focus to the Perfect One, our heavenly Father. When it's obvious our best efforts and planning aren't good enough, we can shift our perspective to the Source of our true strength.

Our key verse, Psalm 18:32, reminds us: Our own strength isn't enough, but God's is.

We all want to be strong and competent. Yet the Bible suggests we should embrace our weaknesses as a reminder to trust in God's strength alone. Paul gave us a picture of the perfection of our weakness when he said, "And He has said to me, 'My grace is sufficient for you, for power is perfected in weakness.' Most gladly, therefore, I will rather boast about my weaknesses, so that the power of Christ may dwell in me" (2 Corinthians 12:9 NASB).

I'm learning to embrace chaos as a sweet call from God to rest in Him when my own work falls short.

Striving for perfection is exhausting. But God waits for us to give in and step aside. Once I end my pursuit of perfection, God can begin His perfecting work in me. We're unable to create perfection, but God makes our way perfect.

What does it look like in everyday life to exchange my weakness for God's strength? To choose His way over my way?

It's trusting Him, rather than trusting my own capabilities.

It's surrendering the pictures of perfection that I carry around in my head to the presence of God in my imperfect reality.

It's walking in daily obedience to His Word and direction, rather than charting my own course. God works powerfully in the midst of our weakness to show His power as we trust, surrender and obey. That's when His strength and perfect way is displayed most brightly in our lives.

Lord, I know if I surrender to You I don't have to be strong all by myself. Instead of sinking into my tangled circumstances, will You teach me to draw on Your strength? In Jesus' name, amen.

REFLECT AND RESPOND:

If you're in a chaotic time of life, write a prayer of trust, surrender and obedience straight from your heart to God.

....

....

....

....

....

....

If you're in a peaceful time of life, write a prayer to God asking Him to prepare you for the next time all doesn't go as planned. Decide now how to react when that time comes.

....

....

....

....

....

....

....

....

....

Day 14: When Worship Makes No Sense • SUZIE ELLER

"Christian brothers, I ask you from my heart to give your bodies to God because of His loving-kindness to us. Let your bodies be a living and holy gift given to God. He is pleased with this kind of gift. This is the true worship that you should give Him." (Romans 12:1 NLV)

The book of Romans stumps me. It doesn't make sense. Honestly.

It was written during the hardest part of Paul's life, a time when he was in jail and he had done nothing wrong. He wrote when the church people who once applauded him now plotted to kill him or waited in the streets, tearing their cloaks in rage because they couldn't stone him.

It puzzles me because it is filled with sayings like "nothing can separate me from God's love," and "my brothers, consider it all joy when you encounter trials." It is a book of hope, of joy, and of life. Yet Paul wrote it from such a place of darkness.

Paul was a real person, not a superhero. What did he discover during those hard times that prompted such rich writings? I think the treasure is found in today's key verse, Romans 12:1. He was a worshipper. I know he sang songs because Scripture shows him singing at the top of his lungs when he was in jail. I don't think, however, that Paul is limiting this to a hymn. It became a way of life. In spite of the dark places, he looked toward the Light, and there he found joy.

Ten years ago a drunk driver slammed into my son. I stood in the church several days after the wreck. I had a bag packed in my car, prepared to go back to my son as soon as service was over. I was weary. I felt helpless. I had come to church only because my husband made me.

"Babe, you have to have a break," he said, promising to stay by Ryan's side.

My son was in pain and had months ahead to heal. The drunk driver had passed away, leaving behind only an underinsured policy that left us with piles of hospital bills and debt.

I grieved for my son. I grieved for the drunk driver's family. I grieved for the loss of normalcy. I grieved—period.

All I knew to do was to raise my hands and lift my face. Tears washed down my cheeks. I wasn't praising God because of my darkness, but because He was the only Light I knew to reach for.

"God, I don't know what the future holds. I don't know how we are going to make it. But I know You."

It was both a physical act—raising my hands—and an act of the heart. I climbed into my Abba Father's arms and wept out of gratefulness. I danced on the inside though there were no dancing shoes in sight.

I thought Romans confuses you, Suz.

That's what I love about it best. In the natural it makes no sense, but supernaturally I totally get it. Darkness holds no power when I hold on to the Light. How can I help but worship Him when I discover that immense truth?

Dear Father, I pray for my sister who feels discouraged, overwhelmed, or lost. I worship You, for

You are our Light in the darkness. You see her and rejoice in her faith, even faith as small as a mustard seed but large enough when placed in Your hands. In Jesus' name, amen.

REFLECT AND RESPOND:

It's not wrong to acknowledge the darkness. It's there. It's tangible.

It's also not wrong to open the door, to flip the light switch to on, to open the shades and let the light come in.

Paul paints it as a physical act. It's overriding feelings to step into truth.

It is a gift to God, but ultimately it is a gift to you, also, as the light blankets the darkness.

Day 15: God Is Not Worried • KAREN EHMAN

"You can go to bed without fear; you will lie down and sleep soundly. You need not be afraid of sudden disaster or the destruction that comes upon the wicked, for the LORD is your security."
(Proverbs 3:24-26a NLT)

As a little girl I loved being outdoors. I could often be found playing kickball with the neighborhood kids or riding my bike around the block. I liked to splash in puddles and jump in piles of leaves. There was one aspect, however, about being outside that I didn't particularly care for: the critters.

Spiders were scary, dogs terrifying. And I couldn't even bear the thought of snakes. My intense fear of these creatures often kept me from fully engaging in play.

Unfortunately, even when I didn't encounter creepy-crawlies outdoors, they occasionally wound up in my dreams at night. I would have the same recurring nightmare of snakes slithering toward me while I stood frozen, unable to run away. When I would wake up, I would be in a panic, heart wildly beating, palms sweating. I never thought my fears would go away until the one summer when I had no other choice.

The summer I turned 20, I took a job at a nature center teaching four-year-olds. It didn't cross my mind that keeping company with critters would be a part of my duties.

I had to capture insects to examine and release, scoop tadpoles to study pond life, and even hold the snakes that were kept in glass tanks in the main building.

Although everything in me wanted to run away, there were little eyes on me. So, I whispered a prayer for strength, pushed past my fears, and made those kids think I was a critter-lovin' instructor whose calm demeanor (and lack of screaming!) showed them there was nothing to fear. If their teacher wasn't freaking out, why should they?

Even though I worked through my fear that summer, as an adult now, I'm still tempted to "freak out" with fear. My imagination concocts all sorts of scenarios peppered with dread and doom. Sometimes I can't shake fear as I try to fall asleep.

But I have come to trust this perspective-shifting truth: God is not worried. He's not in heaven wringing His hands, wondering just how everything will eventually turn out. He is in control. He is loving.

God longs to use the circumstances of our lives to mold our mind, craft our character, and chase away the fears that threaten to slither in, paralyzing us and rendering us ineffective. Ever the patient and wise teacher, if He isn't freaking out, why should we?

Proverbs 3:24-26a is a sweet promise to us, "You can go to bed without fear; you will lie down and sleep soundly. You need not be afraid of sudden disaster or the destruction that comes upon the wicked, for the LORD is your security" (NLT).

Now that passage doesn't promise that we won't ever encounter sudden disasters in life. But it does reassure us that we have no need to fear them. Why? Because the Lord—our gracious and wise teacher—is our security. He will be there to comfort and to guide as He teaches us the lessons we need to learn.

With God as our security, we can have calm in our present. With God as our security, we can face the future without fear. And we can share this confidence we gain to inspire others, helping to keep them from unnecessary fret and worry.

Why it even helps me deal with little critters that get inside my house without squirming. Well... without squirming too much.

Dear Lord, help me place my fears in Your hands, knowing You alone are my security, both now and in the future. In Jesus' name, amen.

REFLECT AND RESPOND:

What is your greatest recurring fear?

....

....

....

Turn it into a prayer by asking God to be your security in the midst of uncertainty.

....

....

....

....

....

....

....

Day 16: How to Sleep Worry Free • AMY CARROLL

"But Jesus called the children to him and said, 'Let the little children come to me, and do not hinder them, for the kingdom of God belongs to such as these.'" (Luke 18:16 NIV)

A friend looked deep into my eyes and asked, "What do you miss about being a child?" In the middle of playing a silly game of questions with a group, the room faded away and memories of my childhood popped into my mind like bubbles surfacing from deep waters.

Playing with my brother in our tree house.

Fun Fridays with my favorite teacher at school.

Riding my banana-seat bike down the street with friends.

Most precious moments snuggled between my parents while our family read together at night.

Although it sounds idyllic, it wasn't perfect. Just like I'm an imperfect parent, my parents weren't perfect either. But as a child I felt loved, encouraged and most importantly, safe and carefree.

As I longed for the feeling of safety that blanketed my childhood, I looked at my friend and answered, "I miss having no worries."

Being an adult is fraught with pits of peril—financial shortfalls, job instability, parenting challenges, marriage conflict, and the general stress of being responsible for yourself and others. For me, childhood was free of all those things. But that day, as I faced my friend's question, adulthood felt like a heavy weight.

The next day as I sat in the quiet of early morning, God whispered a single word into my heart: trust. He gently showed me the weight of adulthood I had shouldered. He nudged me to consider the hours I'd spent awake staring into the dark ruminating, with no resolution. He refreshed the sense of deep longing I'd felt the day before when I'd expressed my desire for childhood. The good old days of no worries.

And He called me back.

Trust is the mark of a child. Of course I had little girl concerns when I was young, but why didn't I feel the weight of worry? It was because I trusted my parents. They took the weight of responsibility to shelter me—allowing me to feel safe and worry-free.

Although not all parents do this well, protecting our children from adult problems is still part of a parent's job description.

The funny thing is my trust was partially based on illusion. As parents, my husband and I have tried to do exactly what my parents did for me. We don't tell our kids about adult problems because we don't want them to worry about things they can't fix.

It's not that we don't have problems or that we're completely in control. The truth is, we're not in control. But there's good news for those who are faking control while lying awake at night and for those who have never felt safe.

God is a Father who is entirely trustworthy because He is truly in control.

As God's children, we have a heavenly Father who is worthy of trust. All our obsessive worry over our responsibilities and concerns doesn't change a thing, so let's resolve to try something different. Let's give up our illusion of control and rest peacefully like children in Jesus' unfailing care.

Now, instead of letting worry consume my nighttime thoughts, I'm learning to pray childlike prayers. I lay in the dark handing over my worries one by one to my faithful Father instead of grasping them in my powerless hands. I'm still in the process of training myself to trust, but I'm sleeping well at night while the One who never slumbers carries it all.

Lord, I've shouldered my cares as if I'm the one in control. Help me become like a child, handing all my stresses, worries and responsibilities to You, my faithful Father. I trust You. In Jesus' name, amen.

- -

REFLECT AND RESPOND:

What worries and responsibilities fill your thoughts and keep you awake at night? Write them on a list.

....

....

....

Reflect a moment. How has your worry changed the situations on your list?

....

....

....

....

....

....

Before bed tonight, pray through your worry list and hand each burden to God. Tell your heavenly Father you trust Him with each one.

Day 17: Great Faith • MICCA CAMPBELL

"Then Jesus answered, 'Woman, you have great faith! Your request is granted.'" (Matthew 15:28 NIV)

I used to covet others' faith. I'd watch the spiritual "giants" in my church and community and wonder why they were given a greater faith than me. It didn't seem fair. Even worse were people with great faith who never seemed to have any type of adversity. Do you know the kind of people I'm describing?

One day I decided to get to know a person with obvious, great faith. I think it was one of the best things I've done to increase my own faith. The first thing I learned was people with great faith got it from their abundance of trials, not from their lack of trials. Trusting God in one trouble gave them courage to trust Him in another. Before they knew it, they had developed great faith in God. Great faith didn't happen overnight; it was a process.

Through the course of trusting God, we discover several things about great faith. First, it leads to great undertakings. Take the Gentile woman with a demon-possessed daughter found in Matthew 15—pause to read her story if you can. She cried out for Jesus to heal her daughter, but she received no response.

This action on Christ's part can seem confusing, so it's important to know that this woman was not only a Gentile, but was of Canaanite descent. The Canaanites were an immoral people God had commanded Israel to completely destroy during their invasion of Canaan under the command of Joshua. Israel did not fully obey God's order and some Canaanites survived the invasion. This woman was their descendant. Nonetheless, this didn't stop her from appealing to Jesus for mercy and help.

Annoyed by her attempts, the disciples urged Jesus to send her away. She was a nuisance to them, but to Jesus the woman was an example of great faith. She was determined to do whatever was necessary to get what she needed.

Great faith also brings about great expectations. If you're like me, you often don't expect great results from your labors and prayers. This is because we lack faith. This was not true of the Gentile woman—she expected the Savior to heal her daughter.

That's not all. Great faith awakens great earnestness. This woman didn't play by the rules. She didn't care what others thought about her actions. Crying, she fell at the feet of Jesus and worshipped Him. I've seen this kind of earnestness in others with great faith as well. They pray with persistence until God moves.

Great faith conquers great difficulties. The woman kept on pursuing Jesus, begging even though He reminded her of her position as a Gentile, not a Jew. Christ responded to her request, "It is not right to take the children's bread and toss it to their dogs" (v.26). In other words, why should He give her, a Gentile, what He had come to give the Jews?

Her answer to that was to agree with Him, "Yes, Lord." And then throw herself on His mercy again by adding, "…even the dogs eat the crumbs that fall from their master's table" (v. 27). She understood that even one morsel of God's power was more than enough to heal her daughter. Pleased with her faith, Jesus commended her.

Finally, great faith achieves great victories. Jesus rewarded the woman's faith by healing her daughter. Our difficulties can be overcome by expressing great faith in Christ's mercy and love, which provide for our needs.

Great faith isn't given to some and not to others. It is a choice we make to trust and pursue God even when at first there appears to be no response.

Dear Lord, my circumstances call for great faith. Today, I'm ready to undertake whatever I need to do in this situation. I expect You to hear and respond to all my concerns. With earnestness, I promise to seek Your will in this area so that I may be more than a conqueror. Victory is already mine because I trust in You. In Jesus' name, amen.

REFLECT AND RESPOND:

Do you ask God to provide for a need and then try to take care of it yourself? If so, why?

....

....

....

....

....

....

Do you think following the example of the Gentile woman will increase your faith?

....

....

....

....

....

Day 18: When I'm Not There, God Is • GLYNNIS WHITWER

"For he will command his angels concerning you to guard you in all your ways." (Psalm 91:11 NIV)

I watched the weather report with heightened concern. A winter snowstorm in the White Mountains was normally great news. It meant the ski lifts would soon be open and that our dry state would benefit from moisture. Today, however, it had a more ominous meaning, for my son Dylan was in the path of the storm.

Dylan and his high school wrestling team had been at a tournament in the mountains for a few days. They were due to be leaving soon, and my concern turned to dread as I pictured those desert dwellers trying to navigate through a snowstorm. My panicked mind reviewed all the horror stories of school sports teams, in vans or buses, going off the road. As I imagined the curving road with blinding snow, my heart started to pound.

The ringing of the phone jarred me from my unhealthy thoughts, and I heard my son's voice on the other end. "Mom," he said. "We're leaving right now to try and beat the storm." I breathed a prayer of thanks for those coaches who cared more about the kids' safety than finishing the tournament, but my worry continued.

Never before had I experienced such a longing to have my son safe in my arms. But that wasn't possible. Dylan had to make that journey home in the care of others. Thankfully, in the midst of my worry, God reminded me that Dylan wasn't just in the care of those coaches, but He was watching over Dylan.

I've struggled with this issue of worry over my children's safety since they were born. Because of my tendency to worry, I have the potential to be overprotective. However, years ago, God revealed to me that my fears were born more out of my lack of trust than a healthy concern. The truth was I believed my children were only safe when they were in my care. The reality of this fallen world is my children are only safe in the care of God.

Many of us will deal with anxiety over our children's safety, as well as countless other things. Instead of being overcome with worry, I've learned to identify the worries that come when I've misplaced my trust. It prompts me to pray more, trust more, and enjoy more of life with my children. By the way, my son and his wrestling team made it home safely that day and my prayer life has been stronger ever since.

Dear Heavenly Father, thank You for caring for my children even more than I do. Thank You for hearing my prayers, and for protecting my children. Help me to learn to trust You more, and to pray more about even the smallest details of their lives. I want to be a woman and mom who trusts You, the true source of all help. In Jesus' name, amen.

REFLECT AND RESPOND:

Make a list of the times when you are most concerned for your child's safety. Commit to praying every day for a week regarding these specific needs. Hopefully this will jumpstart a pattern of consistent prayer. If you aren't currently parenting a child at home, identify a child you know and pray for him or her.

Why is it important for a parent (or any adult) to pray for children?

....

....

....

....

....

....

....

....

....

According to Psalm 91, from what does God protect His people?

....

....

....

....

....

....

....

....

....

Day 19: 'Fraidy Cat • SUZIE ELLER

"For God has not given us a spirit of fear, but of power and of love and of a sound mind."
(2 Timothy 1:7 NKJV)

I stood on the edge of the cliff, the slender bar clenched in my hands. An old chant came to mind as I glanced past the rocky threshold to the thin strips of smoke wisping above two live volcanoes. 'Fraidy cat. 'Fraidy cat.

I was in El Salvador working with children orphaned by previous civil wars. Kings Castle was their sanctuary, and after a hard day's work several children and a counselor had pulled me and others up the cliff with stunning views.

"Jump!" they shouted. The children pointed to the volcanic crater below, its depths inviting but very frightening. The children pointed to a circling boat below, trying to assure me. Then, one after another, children grabbed the bars and flung themselves away from the cliffs, letting go and plunging into the water below.

I looked over at my fellow team members. One shook her head vigorously. "Uh uh," she insisted. I grabbed the bar, noting that my knees were quaking. I closed my eyes, pushed off and swung through the air, screaming when I let go and plunged downward. I hit the icy cold water with a splash. Several children above me shouted and clapped their approval. But I could barely hear them over my own whoops of delight.

I wasn't afraid of jumping that day nearly as much as I was afraid of the unknown. There were elements that were familiar, like water and diving, but when you toss in heights and volcanoes, it knocked me right out of my comfort zone.

Sometimes parenting teens is like that. When my three children moved from tweens to teens, suddenly things changed. There were familiar elements, but lots of scary new developments like driving, dating, and requests for freedom. I wanted to cling to the familiar. I'm the boss, so that's just the way it is. I don't care if everyone else has a later curfew, yours isn't changing.

One day I noticed that my oldest daughter, Leslie, had shut me out, and it hurt. She was 16 years old and I couldn't have been more proud of her. I treasured our relationship, and so was confused by her silence. I finally found the root of her problem. It was me. I was parenting out of fear. 'Fraidy cat. 'Fraidy cat.

I said no to her, not because of her character or the trust she had earned, but because I feared poor influences, or letting her go and her free-falling. I saw some of the teens that used to frequent our home making life-altering decisions, and it shook me. So I pulled her in closer, tighter. I refused to let go—even an inch.

Though I had worked with thousands of teens over 20 years, I made a huge mistake with my own. I forgot to parent Leslie based on who she was, and what I knew to be true, and allowed fear to dictate our relationship instead.

Worse, I made her feel that she was untrustworthy.

That day I stepped up the scary cliff of parenting a teen and took a second look around. I noted the familiar. Leslie had made good decisions. She was maturing, growing into a woman. She wasn't perfect, but she tried really hard to do the right thing, not for me, but because of her faith and her own convictions.

Sometimes parenting is scary. Sometimes letting go a little bit at a time feels uncomfortable, but it's also a key ingredient in shaping our teens into confident adults of character.

But what if they break the trust? Pull the reins back in. Allow them to take responsibility for their mistakes. Then allow them to earn the trust back.

Today Leslie is a 28-year-old married woman, an attorney, and soon-to-be-momma. I wish that I could say that I never faced fear again as a parent, but that simply wouldn't be true. But I learned to recognize fear for what it is—an ineffective response that distorts reality and clouds the decision-making process. Stepping back and looking at the whole picture allowed me to say yes to the opportunities to grow—opportunities for me as a parent, and for my teen.

Dear Lord, help me to see my child clearly today. If I need to set boundaries, help me to set them with love and wisdom. If it is time to encourage my child to grow, to stretch, give me the courage to let go. Thank You for my child's destiny. Thank You that You have a plan for my teen's life. I trust in that today. In Jesus' name, amen.

REFLECT AND RESPOND:

Has your teen proved trustworthy in the past?

If the answer is yes, what are your fears?

....

....

Is there information that would calm those fears (where the teen will be, who they will be with)?

If the answer is no, when were they last untrustworthy and on what scale?

....

....

....

If it has been a long time, are you willing to release the reins a little, with the understanding that additional trust can be earned?

....

....

....

Day 20: No One Is Beyond the Reach of Truth • LYSA TERKEURST

"...I will not venture to speak of anything except what Christ has accomplished through me..."
(Romans 15:18a NIV)

I'm more convinced than ever that people don't care to hear about our Jesus these days until they meet the reality of Jesus in our lives.

Don't skim past that last sentence too quickly. Our history with Jesus is our most effective salvation message to share with others.

If you look at the word 'history,' it's interesting to break it in half and see the words, "His story." That's the thing this world is dying to hear—how His story has been woven into our story. People can debate and argue theology all day long but they can't argue what Jesus has done personally in our lives. Truth lived out is the best sermon.

And while I find people are a little more receptive at Christmas to talking about Jesus, I still find it stressful sometimes with friends and family members. Do you? I think it's important to think about. We've all got people in our lives who need us to break past our hesitations and share the reality of Jesus.

I was profoundly reminded of this years ago when I spoke at a Pregnancy Care Center dinner in Florida. At the end of the night, the center's director asked a board member to come forward and close the evening in prayer. I almost fell out of my chair when I saw this board member was a guy I'd known in high school.

Well, let me clarify that. I knew who he was. He didn't have a clue who I was.

He had been in the uber popular crowd—star athlete who dated the beautiful girls. I was one of those girls in high school who was easy to miss. I felt sort of invisible back then. And judging by the blank look on his face when I made the connection we'd graduated the same year, my assessment was pretty accurate.

He apologized profusely for his wild behavior in high school and acknowledged that he could have been voted, "Least likely to grow up to be a pastor." I agreed. But then again, I wasn't exactly on the fast track toward ministry back then either.

After we chatted for a few minutes, he got a very serious look on his face. Then he said something I won't soon forget.

"You know what is really odd, Lysa? All those years of high school and college, I was a very visible person. I had lots of friends. Then I got a college scholarship to play basketball at a major university and there were even more people who knew me. But no one—no family member, no peer, no girlfriend, no teacher, no coach, no professor, no fan—no one—not one person ever told me about Jesus. All those years, all those people, and not one time did someone try to tell me the truth. Finally when I was twenty-one years old, someone took that chance to share with me how they met Jesus and it radically changed my life."

His statement startled me. And I hope it startles me the rest of my life.

No one is beyond the reach of truth.

Not the wispy, invisible girl who thinks of herself as nothing more than a little background noise. And not the star athlete revered by thousands.

Everyone deserves to hear about Jesus sooner rather than later.

And we must never assume that surely someone else would do a much better job than we would.

Who is in your sphere of influence that needs to hear a bit of your HIS–story this week? Don't let Satan whisper that this message is meant for other people. It's not. If you read this, it's meant for you sweet sister.

And don't fret trying to figure out how to arrange the perfect situation to connect with that person that came to mind. Just tell Jesus you are willing. He's very capable of handling all the details. Our job is obedience. God's job is results.

Dear Lord, thank You for loving me before I even knew You. Give me Your eyes and Your heart to be able to see anyone who needs to know about You today. And give me the right words and the necessary courage to share with my friends and family members. In Jesus' name, amen.

REFLECT AND RESPOND:

Don't let Satan tell you that this message is meant for other people.

Who could you share your story with this week?

Pray. Seek God for the right words and the right opportunity. Take a step of faith. Trust that God will be glorified.

Day 21: But I Can't See! • LYNN COWELL

"The next day Jesus decided to leave for Galilee. Finding Philip, he said to him, 'Follow me.'"
(John 1:43 NIV)

- -

Illuminating a small circle just in front of our feet, the flashlight provided safety and direction for only our next step as Rose and I took our pre-sunrise walk. Anxiety eventually gave way to comfort as we discussed the day ahead. We knew the light would lead us in the right direction. We just had to take the next step…

Taking the next step is something Jesus recommended a very long time ago. "Come and you will see." "Follow me." These were the words Jesus spoke to the disciples as He called them. He didn't sit them down and reveal what the next three years would hold. He knew they would be overwhelmed; possibly even turn around. He chose to keep it simple. "Follow me" was all He said. Take the next step…

As a teen, I wanted to know my future. Will all my dreams come true? What college will I attend? Will I work in a church; marry a pastor? Will I live in Iowa near my family? Jesus knew the answers to those questions all along. I didn't go to college. I don't work in a church, nor did I marry a pastor. He knew. In wisdom, He chose to reveal only enough light for me to take the next step. Sometimes, I catch myself wishing again that I could see my future. I get wrapped up in fear or worry. Career worries: Will I still have this job in five or ten years? Mom worries: Will my children marry spouses passionate about Jesus? Marriage worries: Will my husband and I enjoy a long retirement together? I can spin around issues that really don't have anything to do with this day, with my next step.

Jesus knows. He knows which answers are "yes" and which ones are "no." He knows when and where to reveal to me my next step. My part is simply to take the next step in obedience.

When I was younger, I did not understand those times when He said "no" were stepping stones to His amazing "yes." I learned in the dark that when I step forward in trust and obedience, blessing is down the path. I also had to learn that even those pathways that held pain were part of the process. They were stepping stones in my journey of choosing obedience over worry, fear and control.

Now, when fear and doubt surface in the dark I silence the "what ifs." I remember Jesus' words, "Follow me," and get back on the path that is flickering just ahead—and simply take the next step…a step of trust. I ask Him what I need to do for just today. I walk away from worry by expressing my concerns to Jesus and trust His ability to take care of each and every step.

Dear Lord, the dark can be frightening. Jesus, sometimes my ability to trust seems so much smaller than the step I need to take. Help me to build a history with You. A history of seeing You will help me trust You over and over and over again. I want that. I put my trust in You. In Jesus' name, amen.

REFLECT AND RESPOND:

What areas in my life feel out of control, like I'm walking in the dark? Do I feel alone or am I aware of God's presence with me?

....

....

....

....

....

Have I had trustworthy people in my life in the past? How have these relationships influenced my ability to trust God?

....

....

....

....

....

Day 22: God's Provision • LYSA TERKEURST

"Command those who are rich in this present world not to be arrogant nor to put their hope in wealth, which is so uncertain, but to put their hope in God who richly provides us with everything..." (1 Timothy 6:17 NIV)

It seems you can hardly turn anywhere today without seeing reminders of economic hardships. During the past couple of years the unemployment rate in our country has been the highest we've seen in 60 years. Friends and family members are suffering due to the loss of jobs, investments gone bad, and cutbacks that seem to be everywhere.

I have a friend who has owned a thriving car dealership for over 30 years. This man and his family have been pillars in their community who are known for their generosity and kind Christian spirits.

This past year though, he declared bankruptcy and literally lost everything—including their cars. If that isn't cruel irony, I don't know what is.

So, I've had to have some discussions with God about the absolute heartbreak of this situation. I know God is the great provider, so why isn't He providing for my friend? God is a miracle worker, so why isn't He working a miracle for my friend?

These are fair questions about what seems like a terribly unfair situation.

Whenever I face situations I am having a hard time understanding, I have to park my mind with what I know to be true. Keeping my mind saturated with truth, keeps Satan from being able to whisper dangerous assumptions, false accusations, and faith-eroding perspectives.

So, what is true in this situation? What is true no matter what situation we are facing?

God is a good provider.

This is true. This is where I must park my mind. This is the reality that must saturate my thoughts. This truth rises above our troubling circumstances and calls us to see life from a perspective outside our screaming realities.

God richly provides us with everything we need. Therefore I must trust that God is providing for my friend. What is in front of my friend is God's provision. God hasn't stopped providing just because my friend is in financial turmoil. This situation hasn't caught God off guard. God hasn't run out of resources to help my friend.

Part of God's perfect provision for my friend is to walk through this. I may not like it. I may not understand it. But, because my friend knows and loves God, I have peace that he will make it through this.

The Bible tells us in Philippians 4:8-9 that if we think on what is true, the peace of God will be with us. And ultimately, isn't peace what we want? That's what I really want for my friend. I want this precious man and his family to have peace more than I want their dealership to be saved, their finances restored, and their old life to suddenly come back and settle into place.

Praise God, His peace is but an utterance of truth away. So, sweet sister, park your mind with His truth today. And watch God's perfect provision of peace flood whatever dry and lacking ache you are experiencing right now.

Dear Lord, thank You for being my provider each day. Help me not to fear these times of hardship. Rather, help me to trust in You and Your ways more each day. My desire is to focus on what is true and believe that You will make the rough places smooth. In Jesus' name, amen.

REFLECT AND RESPOND:

Every time a discouraging thought comes into your mind today replace it with a verse from God's Word. Replace it with the truth that God is a good provider and that His unfailing love for you will not be shaken. Replace it by seeking Him and calling on Him for He is always near. How can God's peace restore you today?

Day 23: Believing Is Seeing • MICCA CAMPBELL

"O, LORD, open his eyes so he may see." (2 Kings 6:17a NIV 1984)

When I became a single mom after the death of my first husband, I found my world turned upside down. My life was a balancing act of finances, home and being a stabilizing factor in my son's life.

Decisions that needed to be made closed in on me, but there was no one to consider them with. Which bills had to be paid first? Should I work outside the home? What's the best school for my son?

The more I tried to figure it out, the more afraid I became. Most of the time I avoided the pressing worry and doubt by curling up and sleeping. The burden was huge and the enemy of fear surrounded me.

I felt backed into a corner, tired, worn out and alone.

The truth is, I may have felt alone, but I wasn't. God was there. I knew I had to turn my attention on Him instead of my circumstances. I knew God wouldn't let me fall. I knew He was aware and cared about my worries. So I called on Him for help and asked Him to open my eyes so I might see His provision. I prayed:

"Lord, I trust You are with me. I know You will never leave me nor forsake me. I am not alone. You care for me. You are my provider and You have a perfect plan for me. I do not have to be afraid, for You are faithful."

My prayer ended by asking God to open my eyes so I could see what I had prayed for and professed with my mouth.

He did that for Elisha and his friend in 2 Kings 6:17. King Aram was at war with Israel. During this time, the prophet Elisha and another man of God continuously spied on King Aram and reported his strategy to the king of Israel. When King Aram found out Elisha was the one blowing his cover to Israel, he sent horsemen and chariots by night to surround Elisha's camp and capture him.

When Elisha and the man of God woke up and saw they were encircled by the enemy, the man of God cried out in terror, "What shall we do?" (2 Kings 6:15 NIV 1984) Elisha responded, "Do not be afraid. For those who are with us are more than them" (2 Kings 6:16 NIV 1984).

Then Elisha called to the Lord, "Open his eyes so he may see" (2 Kings 6:17a). Suddenly, the man of God saw chariots of fire from God all around. What do you think that did to his fear to know that God was fighting the battle for them?

Do doubt, fear, worry and discouragement surround you? Do you fear they will conquer you? Are you crying out like Elisha's friend, "What am I going to do?" Day by day I committed to face my fears by focusing on God and His power. He guided me with each decision I had to make.

Perhaps it's time to ask God to open your eyes to see His power and love working together to fight your battle. Seeing the truth will help you take a step toward freedom and away from fear. He is in the midst of your circumstances.

Dear Lord, it's hard to trust when I'm afraid. But I choose to look to You and believe You are working on my behalf. Help me to see You in the midst of my cares. In Jesus' name, amen.

REFLECT AND RESPOND:

Begin to face your fears and take action. Set aside time to pray, asking the Lord to show you His power in the challenges you're facing.

As you watch Him work on your behalf, mark each challenge off one at a time. You'll discover that with God's help you're more courageous than you imagined.

Day 24: Dare to Hope • WENDY POPE

"Yet I still dare to hope when I remember this." (Lamentations 3:21 NLT)

Have you ever cried until the tears would no longer come and your heart was broken in tiny pieces? Have you ever uttered, "Everything I hope for from the Lord is lost"? Then you, me, and Jeremiah make three.

I won't ever forget those long nights of crying myself to sleep. Some nights only silent tears would fall; other nights loud wails accompanied questions and prayers. "Why Lord? What am I doing wrong? Why won't you just fix his problems?" The prayers would end with "if it is Your will," hoping that His will was different that what it appeared to be.

On these nights I would curl up in a ball under my covers, face the wall and hope this time there would be a breakthrough in my prayers. Many nights, as I cried myself to sleep, I believed everything I had hoped for was lost and the situation was hopeless.

Jeremiah, also known as the weeping prophet, found himself in a hopeless situation as he watched the Temple of the Lord being burned to the ground by the Babylonians. His heart broke. The elements of the Temple such as the water basin and lamp snuffers were stolen, taken to Babylon to be used to worship false gods.

Jeremiah prophesied God's words to the people of Judah and Jerusalem. The Lord's immediate future for His people was one of discipline and the utter destruction of Jerusalem as well as His holy Temple. Jeremiah was chosen by God to deliver these words to His people. He did his job and did it well, but not without punishment, ridicule, insults, and imprisonment.

Jeremiah cried until no more tears would come (Lamentations 2:11 NLT). His heart was broken for Jerusalem and for God's people, his people. In anguish he lamented the words, "Everything I had hoped for from the Lord is lost" (Lamentations 3:18 NLT).

Then, out of the midst of his despair, he dared. He dared to hope in what he remembered. Many of us know someone who needs hope; perhaps we ourselves need hope, therefore it would serve us well today to know what Jeremiah remembered. What he remembered as he lamented gave him the courage to dare to hope again. The remembrance changed his perspective on his present situation. Jeremiah dared to hope and so can we, regardless of our circumstances. In reading Lamentations 3:21-24 you can hear the expression in Jeremiah's "voice" change from that of lament to that of optimism. In your mind's eye you can picture his facial features transforming. What Jeremiah remembered was the key to elevating him from the pit of despair to a place of expectancy. It is our key as well. Jeremiah remembered this about his covenant Lord:

• His unfailing love for him

• His new mercies meant for him

• His never ending faithfulness toward him

• His inheritance due to him

God's Word is alive and active. It is designed to transform us from the inside out. Reading and applying its truths will change the expression in our voice and redirect our perspective for the future. During my desperate nights I longed for my circumstances to be different. I cried until the tears would no longer come. Many times I tarried in the pit of despair much longer than necessary. But when I remembered God's faithfulness and mercies to me, my expression changed.

Did the circumstances surrounding my sorrows change because I remembered? No. What changed was my outlook. Hope means to wait with expectation, and this is what I chose to do during those hard nights.

Are you in need of hope today? Will you choose to remember His faithfulness, love, and mercy despite the despair and destruction around you? Will you dare to hope?

Dear Lord, I want to dare to hope but life around me seems uncertain and tentative. Will You help me dare to hope? Will You help me remember Your faithfulness, love and mercy? Thank You in advance for what You are going to do. In Jesus' name, amen.

REFLECT AND RESPOND:

Read Lamentations 3:21-24 aloud. Remember and write down God's expressions of faithfulness, mercy, and love to you. Dare to hope. Forward today's devotions to someone who needs hope.

....

....

....

What is my biggest stumbling block that keeps me from daring to hope?

....

....

....

What is an area of my life in which I need to dare to hope?

....

....

....

Day 25: What If I Fall? • TRACIE MILES

"Remember, it is sin to know what you ought to do and then not do it." James 4:17 (NLT)

It seemed like a great idea at first, until my fear and procrastination caused me to miss a blessing.

I'd been invited to speak at a summer camp and my daughter Kaitlyn joined me. In between attending the worship events, we were given the opportunity to sign up for outdoor activities, one of which was a ropes and zip line course dangling high in the mountain trees.

After putting on safety gear and listening to basic instructions, Kaitlyn and I waited our turn in line. Yet while she was filled with excitement, dread filled my heart.

I watched each girl clip her carabineer and climb up the towering tree to the first platform landing. My heart raced and my inner voice of reason worked overtime. What was I thinking? Why would anyone want to climb all the way up there, just for fun? What if I get up there and I'm too scared to get back down? What if I can't finish the course and get embarrassed? What if my rope breaks and I fall?

The more I procrastinated, the more people moved ahead and the more I convinced myself I could not accomplish this task. Finally it was my turn. I started up the tree. Slowly. Hesitantly. Fearfully. I looked down the entire time, though the camp leaders constantly encouraged me to look up instead. After just a few moments, I caved into all those irrational fears, climbed down the tree and removed my safety gear.

Later, I watched Kaitlyn climb high into the treetops, safely attached to the ropes, moving from platform to platform. I regretted my procrastination and fear of taking a risk. As the wind rustled through her long blonde hair and the sun shone on her face, she smiled and hollered down how beautiful the view was from high above. As she zoomed down the zip line and splashed into the lake water below, I could sense the accomplishment and joy that washed across her face.

And then I realized I'd missed the blessing of experiencing something new—seeing the beauty of the forest from a higher view instead of my limited view from the ground. Unfortunately, that wasn't the first time I'd let fear and procrastination interfere with God's blessings in my life.

Jesus knew we would struggle with procrastination. He gave us truths in His Word to combat it. But in today's key verse we also see that not doing what we feel called to do is not only procrastination, but sin.

When God calls us to make a "risky" move for Him, we often worry and try to reason ourselves out of it. We might spend time looking at our obstacles rather than at God, which makes courage flee and fear paralyze us. In fact, when we wait for every life circumstance to be perfect before we step out in faith, the devil is happy to spend his time trying to bring us down and convince us to never move at all.

Procrastination may seem to come normal for us, but it is never God's best for us. We don't often think of it as sin, but anytime we don't do what God calls us to do, when He calls us to do it, it is sin. It's easier said than done, but we mustn't let fear outweigh faith.

Jesus encourages us to fulfill the work He called us to do and not to waste time procrastinating. Not simply because it's a sin, but because time is precious, and He promises that obedience brings blessings. How sad to miss the abundant blessings that come when we follow God's call, simply because we keep putting it off.

Not pushing past my fears to a zip line obviously was not sin, but not doing what God instructs me to do always is. I've finally learned that when we take a leap of faith, with God, we have everything to gain and nothing to lose but fear.

Father, give me the courage to take a risk for You and the strength to take a leap of faith in whatever You call me to do. In Jesus' name, amen.

REFLECT AND RESPOND:

Write two things God's prompted you to do that you procrastinated in obeying. Pray for God's strength and courage to act.

....

....

....

What is one step you can take this week to push past procrastination?

....

....

....

....

....

....

Day 26: You Get to Decide • RENEE SWOPE

"We demolish arguments and every pretension that sets itself up against the knowledge of God, and we take captive every thought to make it obedient to Christ." (2 Corinthians 10:5 NIV)

My eight-year-old son walked into my room before school one morning and declared, "Mom, I don't want to have any anxious thoughts today!

"I don't want to worry about you not being home when I get off the school bus. I don't want to worry about my teacher not liking my science project. And I don't want to worry about Dad getting in a car accident! I wish I could be like other kids because they never worry."

Listening to him describe his fears made my stomach ache. Anxious thoughts had been a companion ever since I was a child, so I knew just how he felt.

However, I assumed my fears stemmed from hard things in my childhood during my parents' divorce. My anxiety had solid reasoning behind it. My dad left before I was ever born. And by the time I was 2 years old, their divorce was final.

For as long as I could remember, I feared my mom would leave me too. Fear of rejection and abandonment followed me into every relationship I had for the rest of my life: with friends, boyfriends and even my husband.

Somewhere along the way, I accepted worry as a disability and settled into believing I didn't have a choice in how it impacted my life. I let anxiety form a pattern in my thoughts.

Now here I stood with my son who'd declared he wanted a day off from worry! And I was determined to help him get it. I wanted to rip those threads of fear out of his thoughts and make sure he knew what to do with them.

I couldn't take my child's fears away, but I could equip him with the truth to face them courageously and fight them victoriously. I told Andrew, "You get to decide what to do with your worries." And I shared three powerful truths to help him:

Truth #1: Other kids do worry; they just don't talk about it on the playground.

Truth #2: Worry and fear must be a normal because God tells us not to, over 100 times in the Bible.

Truth #3: God doesn't just tell us not to worry or fear, He tells us what to do when we do!

I read today's verse out loud from 2 Corinthians 10:5, "We demolish arguments and every pretension that sets itself up against the knowledge of God, and we take captive every thought to make it obedient to Christ." But a puzzled look on his face told me Andrew needed to know how to do that, so I described it in terms he could understand:

"Andrew, when you have a thought that makes you feel anxious, you have to decide to catch it like a baseball." I then cupped my hand like I was holding a ball and told him to look at it and ask, "Is this something Jesus would say to me?"

If the answer is "no" — then throw your thought back into the outfield!

For instance, worry says: "Your mom isn't going to be home when you get off the bus."

"Would Jesus say that?" I asked.

"No," he replied.

"Then it's outta here!" I told him, as I threw the invisible ball across the room.

Worry says: "Your teacher isn't going to like your science project!"

"Would Jesus say that?" I prompted.

Again, "No."

"Throw that one away, too!"

We talked through each worry, and I helped him decide what to do. Then we prayed and asked God to replace each worry with confident peace, and thanked God for ways He'd protected Andrew in the past, reminding him how good He is at being God.

After our collective "Amen" I looked up and Andrew had a big grin on his face. Then he said, "Thanks Mom!" as though all his worries were gone.

My sons are 17 and 20 now, and there have been many days I've wanted to take away their worries. I've been tempted to fix problems and sticky situations. But I've learned that doesn't strengthen their faith or their ability to decide what to do when hard times come.

Instead, what our kids need most is for us to be there: to talk through their struggles, listen to their stories, pray through their worries and be willing to share God's truths that have helped us decide how to face ours.

Dear Lord, show me how to be still and listen, and let You be God in my child's life. Help me walk in Your truth and win the war over my own worry so I can share Your Word and show them how to lean on You when they come to me for help. In Jesus' name, amen.

REFLECT AND RESPOND:

How much does fear and worry impact your daily decisions and joy (or your child's)?

....

....

....

What might happen if you took each anxious thought captive and decided which ones stay and which ones go, based on what Renee shared today?

....

....

....

Day 27: *Where Your Treasure Is* • SUZIE ELLER

"Don't store up treasures here on earth, where moths eat them and rust destroys them, and where thieves break in and steal." (Matthew 6:19 NLT)

I was on my own at 17. I worked two jobs while attending a small community college and eventually left college because I ran out of funds. Three years later I married my husband. Over the next few years babies were born, with medical expenses incurred. Then I got sick: Cancer. It probably won't surprise you that because of these circumstances, there was a huge need in my life for financial stability.

I pinched pennies. I calculated paychecks to the last dime. I made lists of our debts month after month, figuring out how to pay them off quicker. I think financial gurus would say I was on the right track, but can I be honest? In the midst of my calculations and my overwhelming need for security, pinching pennies became not just a means to meet my goal and take care of our family, but it started to reflect my heart spiritually in the area of giving.

Even after I was secure. Even after our financial status was stable.

We tithed. We gave to others, even sacrificially. But my heart wasn't in it. As I placed a tithing envelope in the offering, I thought: What about our savings? Shouldn't we be building it? What about buying something new for us? Our car is older. The miles are racking up.

Friends would have been surprised at the battle that raged inside me. I was ashamed of it. They would have called me generous, but I knew the truth. I had worked so hard for such a long time that I had come to count on Suzie. I obeyed God in this area, but did I trust Him?

I desperately wanted a generous heart, no matter how much was in our bank account. The first thing I felt God asking me to lay down was worry. As I prayed, I went back to all the times God had liberally cared for me. As an unsure young girl alone at 17, His love led me day by day. As a young mom overwhelmed at times, He wrapped me in security and grace. As a 31-year-old woman diagnosed with cancer, He filled me with faith that could only come from Christ.

My confidence in Him had nothing to do with money, but rather His presence in my life. I put worry down, asking for the strength to abide in Him instead of fear.

The second thing I felt God asking me to lay down was resentment. Oh, Father, such a hard word. Are You sure that is the condition of my heart? And yet, there it was. Hidden from others, but clear as day to me and my Savior.

It's been years since that pivotal moment between me and Jesus. Recently I was talking with one of my daughters. "Remember when you used to worry about money?" she asked. I nodded, smiling. "You seem to be so different, Mom, and yet I know that you and Dad live on a strict budget, especially now that he's back in school. Do you have money I don't know about?" she teased.

Yes, baby, I do. But it has nothing to do with my bank account. It's a different kind of treasure, one that acknowledges how rich I am to have food on the table, a car that starts every time I turn the key, a family that loves me like crazy, and faith that runs deep. It's a treasure that is nestled inside, that is filled with joy when I drop off books at a shelter, or send a check to sponsor my beautiful Compassion International child, or respond to God's leading to give more than a tithe. It's a treasure that is a deep confidence in who God is.

In many ways I'll always be that 17-year-old girl wanting to be secure, but I've found a different kind of security. I may never be wealthy, but believe me when I say this: I'm rich beyond belief. I'm blessed, blessed, blessed.

Dear Jesus, You see my heart. You know my fears, insecurities, and hunger for stability. I pray I will see the vast riches around me, things others might not see as wealth, but in the end they are the most priceless. In Jesus' name, amen.

REFLECT AND RESPOND:

List the things that money provides for you.

....

....

....

List the things you provide for yourself.

....

....

....

List the things God provides for you.

....

....

....

In each, describe your heart condition. Is it in balance with today's scripture (Matthew 6:19-21)?

....

....

....

Day 28: ...And She Lives Happily Ever After • GLYNNIS WHITWER

"... your eyes saw my unformed body; all the days ordained for me were written in your book before one of them came to be." (Psalm 139:16 NIV)

I had finished reading a bestselling novel that was over 1,000 pages—epic in size and story. It consumed me for weeks. A respected acquaintance recommended it, and once committed, I stuck with it to the end —in spite of wanting to quit, often.

By the end of the first chapter, I realized it wasn't going to be an easy read. The story was set in the Middle Ages, with uncomfortably real sections. Perhaps I'm a bit sheltered, but it seemed to contain unnecessarily graphic descriptions. Skimming over the uncomfortable spots, I kept reading.

The book ended well, but there were times when I was ready to close the cover, and move on to something happier. The antagonists were just too mean. The plot too painful. The abuse, greed and vindictiveness too ugly to dwell on.

If that book ended badly, I would have been disgruntled at spending weeks of my life on it. On the other hand, I would have been frustrated to quit before finishing. Here's why.

If I had quit reading at page 245, the story would have seemed hopeless. I might have thought the villains won, or the hero and heroine never reconnected. If I had read a bit further, to say page 576, the story would have ended with justice as an impossible dream, and hatred and revenge as unavoidable and all-consuming parts of life.

But, after reading the book in its entirety, I could see the amazing story. The plot progressed steadily; there was tension, conflict and eventually resolution. Good did triumph, although not without many bumps along the way.

It got me thinking that our lives are a bit like that. For those of us who have accepted Christ, we will have a happy ending in heaven with God. One way or another, our story will end well. But not every page or chapter in our story is happy.

Today might be page 452 for me. And on page 452 there is conflict and tension. Last year might have been chapter nine. And in chapter nine, the protagonists struggle financially, and wonder why God allowed such pain into their lives. If I only read one page or chapter, I would have a very different view of the story.

Yet the Author of my story has a purpose for every page and chapter in my life. He's got a story in mind and is building and developing the plot every day. No story is conflict-free. No story is complete without a challenge. Victory is empty without a struggle.

Today, I'm considering my life as a grand story. Good will triumph. The victory will be sweeter because of the struggle. Today is not the story. It's just page 452. So I will press on, trusting in a loving and creative Author to bring about resolution. You see, I already know the ending—she lives happily ever after.

Dear Lord, I praise You for Your creative and all-powerful nature. In light of the difficulties I'm facing today, I choose to trust You, believing You are writing an epic story in my life. Help me to press on when I want to give up. In Jesus' name, amen.

REFLECT AND RESPOND:

Day 29: Does God Still Speak to Ordinary People? • GLYNNIS WHITWER

"All this I have spoken while still with you. But the Counselor, the Holy Spirit, whom the Father will send in my name, will teach you all things and will remind you of everything I have said to you." (John 14:25-26 NIV)

The Bible tells amazing stories of God speaking directly to humans. God walked and talked with Adam. He spoke through a burning bush to Moses, and God had direct messages for His people after speaking with the prophets of old. Growing up, I wondered if God had stopped speaking to normal people after Bible times. After all, I never heard Him speak.

Years went by, I matured in my faith, got married, taught Sunday school, sang in the choir, and loved God and His people. But I never heard Him speak to me. Honestly, it didn't bother me much, because I figured God had said all He needed to say, and it was in the Bible. What more did I need to hear?

Apparently, God had something more to say. It wasn't until we moved across country that I discovered He longed to communicate personally with me.

Twelve years ago, my family moved from Phoenix to Charlotte. It wasn't a move I wanted, but I begrudgingly acquiesced to support my husband's dream of living somewhere else. Instead of embracing the adventure, all I saw was loss: my career, church, friends and extended family. I was heartbroken.

It was in that condition I started hearing God "speak" to me. It wasn't in an audible voice, or in any unusual way, just a clear voice in my spirit. One that hadn't been there before. God put scriptures in my mind I didn't know I had memorized. He spoke words of encouragement specifically for me. He gave me direction to do things I never would have done on my own. Here's an example:

We had been church searching for a few weeks when God directed us to a small congregation meeting in a grade school. One week, a lovely young woman gave her testimony. My heart was moved. That very same week, I heard a radio spot by the woman who had spoken at the church. God spoke to me in a way I'd never before experienced and He clearly told me to call her and offer my services as a volunteer.

I was startled, but obeyed. It took a few phone calls, but I finally reached Lysa TerKeurst, the President of Proverbs 31 Ministries.

"Hi Lysa," I said. The next words came tumbling out of my mouth as I blurted, "I've just moved to Charlotte, I saw you at church, then heard you on the radio. I've got a degree in journalism and I'm wondering if you need any volunteers."

There was a pause on the other end of the phone before Lysa answered, "We've been praying for someone with a degree in journalism."

It was exciting to hear God speak to me, and I began to understand what Jesus meant when

He said God the Father would send His Holy Spirit to communicate with us. I saw how God was orchestrating events when I listened to and obeyed His Spirit within me. In a conversation with a friend from home, I told her about this new experience. She said that perhaps my life had been too full to hear God before my move.

She was right, but there was more. I was very independent and made decisions without consulting God. In truth, I hadn't needed Him or His counsel, very much. Or so I thought. It wasn't until everything I depended on was removed that I became empty and desperate for God to fill me. From my place of need, God's Spirit became my counselor, comforter, and guide. Years ago, I asked God for help in this area. I knew I had the potential to slip back into my independent ways, and I wanted to keep hearing His voice. I asked Him to always keep me humble and in need of Him. Although that was a hard prayer to pray, it's even harder to live out because God answered it. If that's the price of hearing God, I'll gladly pay it.

Dear heavenly Father, thank You for speaking to ordinary people through Your Holy Spirit. Forgive me for the times I get busy and independent. I want to hear Your voice above all else. Help me to trim things from my life so there is room for You. In Jesus' name, amen.

REFLECT AND RESPOND:

Spend a few moments in prayer and ask God to speak directly to you. You might ask Him to answer a question or give you direction. When you get an answer, write down this experience and share it with someone else.

....

....

....

....

When do you know the thoughts you have are NOT from God?

....

....

....

How can you open yourself up more to hear God speak?

....

....

....

Day 30: *Being Thankful Changes Everything* • LYSA TERKEURST

"For our struggle is not against flesh and blood, but against the rulers, against the authorities, against the powers of this dark world and against the spiritual forces of evil in the heavenly realms." (Ephesians 6:12 NIV)

I sat on the bed, tears streaming down my face, negative thoughts racing through my mind … Why does marriage have to be so hard sometimes? Why can't he see my side of things? Why won't he change? Maybe I married the wrong man.

This was a scene repeated over and over the first five years of my marriage. I was discouraged, overwhelmed and so tempted to give up. But here I am about to celebrate my 18th wedding anniversary so thankful I didn't walk away.

Ephesians 6:12 was a great reminder to me over the years that my husband isn't my enemy. Art may feel like my enemy but the truth is Satan is the real enemy who hates marriage and schemes against my husband and me. One thing we must always remember is Satan's goal to be one who casts something between two to cause a separation.

Satan wants to separate us in every way. He wants to separate us with conflict, hurt feelings, misunderstanding, and frustrations of all kinds. He wants to separate us from our neighbors, our friends, our co-workers, our parents, our spouses, our kids. He wants to separate us from God's best. He wants to separate us from God.

One of the best ways for Satan to start these separations is by luring us into a place of grumbling and complaining. If he can get us to focus only on what is aggravating and negative in life, then little cracks of distance start forming in our relationships. The grass starts looking greener everywhere else except where we are standing.

I can see this so clearly when I look back on the first five years of my marriage. Somehow, I became so hyperfocused on all I felt was wrong with my husband, I became blinded to all that was good. I grumbled and complained and nagged and set out to change him. And I almost destroyed my marriage in the process. Satan had a field day as the separation between Art and me kept ever widening.

Then one day as I was in a fit of tears asking God to make things better, I felt challenged to start listing out things about Art for which I was thankful.

It was hard at first. I had bought Satan's whispers that there was only negative there with very little positive to find. But, with each positive quality I listed, it slowly changed everything. It was as if the clouds of negativity lifted and I could once again see his good qualities. There were so many good qualities; I was shocked how I'd gotten so blinded.

How sad I spent five years thinking the grass would be greener with someone else. Not true. The grass is always greener where you water and fertilize it. And being thankful—really intentionally listing out things for which we are thankful—is a great way to start watering and fertilizing and changing everything.

Dear Lord, thank You for helping me see how beneficial it is to be aware and appreciative of the good qualities in those I love. Lord, help me to recognize Satan's schemes and combat them with the power of having a truly thankful heart. In Jesus' name, amen.

- -

REFLECT AND RESPOND:

Every time a negative, separating thought comes into your mind today, intentionally combat it with something for which you are thankful about that person.

How does it make you feel to dwell on what you wish was different about another person?

....

....

....

....

....

Could this devotion showing up in your inbox today be a reminder from God that there are positive things for which you can be thankful?

....

....

....

....

....

How does having a thankful heart change things?

....

....

....

....

....

....

Hi there!

My name is Lysa TerKeurst, and I have the honor of leading the staff at Proverbs 31 Ministries.

I work with the most incredible team of women (and one brave man!). But before you get that sinking feeling of not quite measuring up at the mention of the Proverbs 31 woman in the Bible, I think I should quickly admit, me too. Trust me when I say we are simply a group of women sold out to saying yes to God and He truly does the rest.

When I helped start Proverbs 31 Ministries over twenty years ago, I remember thinking this Proverbs 31 woman was perfect. She was someone who had it all together. She actually enjoyed cooking and cleaning. She raised flawless children who never had outbursts. She never had issues with her friends. She stayed balanced with her finances. And she never had hormonal responses with her husband.

I honestly didn't feel like I could measure up.

But I quickly came to realize it wasn't her activity but rather the Proverbs 31 woman's identity that mattered the most.

A Proverbs 31 woman is, at her core, someone who seeks the Lord in everything she does and trusts Him wholeheartedly with her life. The mission behind our ministry is to meet women right where they are in the real, hard places we all experience and to intersect God's Word right there.

Proverbs 31 Ministries provides the biblical perspective for the gut honest issues women face. And, by purchasing this 30-day prayer journal, you're helping us provide free resources to women all around the world.

And when women around the world are changed by God's Word...it means families around the world are being impacted by that change. Thank you for being a catalyst in making change happen!

Sweet blessings,

Lysa TerKeurst
President of Proverbs 31 Ministries

Proverbs 31
MINISTRIES

*She is clothed with strength and dignity;
she can laugh at the days to come.*

PROVERBS 31:25

Proverbs 31 Ministries is a nondenominational, nonprofit Christian ministry that seeks to lead women into a personal relationship with Christ. With Proverbs 31:10-31 as a guide, Proverbs 31 Ministries reaches women in the middle of their busy days through free devotions, daily radio message, speaking events, conferences, resources, online Bible studies, and training in the call to write, speak and lead others.

We are real women offering real-life solutions to those striving to maintain life's balance, in spite of today's hectic pace and cultural pull away from godly principles.

Wherever a woman may be on her spiritual journey, Proverbs 31 Ministries exists to be a trusted friend who understands the challenges she faces, walks by her side, encouraging her as she walks toward the heart of God.

Visit us online today at proverbs31.org!

IF YOU ENJOYED THIS 30 DAY EXPERIENCE
OF DRAWING CLOSE TO GOD,

we think you'll love our First 5 App!

WE SAY WE PUT GOD FIRST. SO WOULDN'T IT MAKE SENSE
TO GIVE HIM THE FIRST 5 MINUTES OF EACH DAY?

WE MUST EXCHANGE

whispers with God

BEFORE

shouts with the world.

LYSA TERKEURST,
President of Proverbs 31 Ministries

Download the app today
BY VISITING THE APP STORE
ON YOUR IPHONE OR ANDROID DEVICE.

*ALSO, USE "GIFT4U" TO RECIEVE $3 OFF YOUR NEXT
EXPERIENCE GUIDE TO ACCOMPANY THE CURRENT STUDY IN THE APP.*

When each day is filled with obligations, unexpected moments, and relationships that sometimes get difficult, it is essential to know you are not alone.

Find a *friend* on the pages of the NIV Real-Life Devotional Bible for Women.

Filled with insightful daily devotions written by Lysa TerKeurst and the Proverbs 31 Ministries team, the devotions in this Bible will meet you where you are—on the good and on the hard days, in the carpool line, or at the doctor's office.

God's truth will help you maintain a peace-filled balance in spite of life's hectic pace.

Features of the Bible:

- The beauty and clarity of the New International Version (NIV) Bible
- 366 devotions that will inspire you to live authentically as a woman of God
- Author biographies
- A helpful subject index

To purchase your Bible visit p31bookstore.com

NOTES

NOTES

NOTES